SPIRITUAL BOOT CAMP

CURE TO GET RID OF YOUR EGO HASSLES FOR GOOD .

ANJANA P BALIGA

Made with ♥ on the Notion Press Platform
www.notionpress.com

I dedicate this book to you, The Reader. Your willingness to awaken your inner self inspires me. Your commitment to working at your absolute best to become the Best Version of yourself moves me.

and your readiness to leave everyone you meet better than you found them encourages me to give even more of my life to help people empower their life's so that they keep Learning Growing and Evolving in their respective fields.

Contents

Preface

As you all, know that "Rome was not built in a day." which means it is not possible to master everything in a day but doing everyday something will definitely build a Masterpiece for you. what will you learn through this book you will get an idea of what is spiritual Retreat looks like. Doing meditation every day will help you to improve your Aura and also will give you positivity to deal with problems and people in your life.

The only way to escape from the prison of fear is action __Joa Tye

Meditation is the real treasure of your life. It is more valuable than any Materialistic Wealth. Each one of us can find inner pleasure and it is very easy to meditate. In fact, there is Nothing to be done in meditation. Just find a quiet and relaxing place where no one can disturb you. You sit on a mat so that you cannot have contact with the earth. Let your back remain straight. Place your arms on your knees facing the sky. Now close your eyes and take some long Deep breaths after that slowly and slowly let the breath return to normal. and Now with your mind keep watching your breath coming in and out. Don't let go even a single breath without watching .... keep inhaling and exhaling watching like a watchman ....in between your mind will wander here and there but keep your focus on the breath. Don't do anything else watching the breath slowly and slowly your breath will slow down ...and your mind will be calm gradually. A moment will come when all the thoughts will disappear your mind will draw into the ocean of peace....

This is the state of deep meditation.

You all can meditate and if you continue this _**practice for 90 days**_ you will see **drastic changes** in your life and then you will feel continuing it all throughout your life. This Is the End of suffering one's life.

Acknowledgements

To God, for his loving guidance, and strength, and for the many blessings he has bestowed upon me forever.

To the Angelic Realm Angels and Archangels who guided me to write this book so that I could bring my idea as a book or legacy to the world.

To my parents and my in_ laws for whatever they have taught me which has served me so well in my life.

To my both sons Aditya and Vinayak & my cat Mimi for their inspirational support all throughout my life.

To my husband, better half Dr. Dinesh Baliga for his source of inspiration and moral support without Whom I could not have reached the desired Heights.

Last but not least Mr. Zubin is an author &trainer and founder of Genius trainers, an online coaching institute.

Under Zubin's guidance, I was able to create my first Kindle eBook and get my book printed through notion press.His online course is easy and practical oriented

He is a great Mentor and a true guide for this project. He teaches people How to be an Author in 7 days.

Introduction

The excitement of Being Human is that we all are different with unique skills and different personalities.

Each one living is in a different place in their soul's evolution and awareness. We came from the Divine and we will return to the Divine before we decided to have this physical experience on earth as Spiritual beings.

We are experiencing existence along with Angels who live in the realm of the heavens about we have come to earth to learn lessons to advance our SOUL development. The earth is like a cosmic theme park where we queue up and go on a number of adventures. There is no lack of opportunity or limit on the ability to incarnate.

We Come to earth for two purposes Global evolution and Personal growth and both must happen in balance when we are born the earth creates the illusion; that separates us from the Divine and the whole life journey is all about knowing who we are and this is only possible if we could get rid of our Ego Hassles for Good.

The book is about a Spiritual Boot Camp which helps all spiritual aspirants to discover the Real Self by letting go of their Fears, Struggle, Guilt & Karmic baggage's etc.

if we experience purity then only, we can transcendent unconditional love.

CHAPTER ONE

Divine Gifts

Yesterday I met Mr. Nair I went to his house for a cup of tea. He had recently visited the Temple of the Monkey God the ANJANEYA TEMPLE He brought the prasadam bag; I was very curious about this bag.

The bag contained a literature book (boot camp), Hanuman Chalisa, a packet of the diyas, Incense sticks, a bottle of Holy water, laddu Prasad and Rudraksha mala. I asked about them he explained they are all the five elements of which the universe is made. BH G V A N (the DIVINE, THE UNIVERSE or what we call as GOD

BH Bhoomi, the earth

G gagan the sky, the space

V Vayu the air

A agni the fire

N neer the water

WE SHOULD ALWAYS BLESS THE WATER, AIR, FIRE, SPACE & THE EARTH.

He said the Prasadam was made from the flour which came from Mother Earth feeling blessed to share the fruits of mother earth; the literature book contains all the details of the Boot camp; the Hanuman Chalisa was to be recited every day (space) and a Bead rosary to chant the Mantra; the incense stick fills the air and purified it with positive

Vibes. Special breath work and some yoga exercises were also taught he further added to our conversation.

The Diyas are a representation of fire elements; help each one to move our souls from darkness to light. The Holy water represents 70% of the water in our bodies. A separate manifestation about how to drink charged water for everyday wellness was also part of the boot camp. I asked about the details and he gave me a link to the Google form to for the two-day BOOT CAMP. program. I was very excited and filled out the Google form. He said that the camp was full of learning all about how to live a fulfilled life

One month before I had booked the train tickets and reached the destination on the desired date.

The Spiritual retreat

I was in awe stuck when I reached the destination the surrounding forest was lush green in the distance, I could see a beautiful waterfall we pass through the small forest cover and they were tall buildings containing our rooms. At the center was a temple of HANUMAN and surrounding the temple area was a path to walk around. There were several rooms in a circular way; the assembly hall, the Annapurna hall, the recreation hall, the library, and the reception.

A bus took us to our rooms and later on took us down to the Annapurna kitchen hall for our dinner. The next day morning we were asked to come to the main hall and the temple area Built during the 19th century the pyramid Valley has its own significance they are known as the center of meditation.

As meditation is the elixir of life and all the answers to our life's sufferings lie within. And to go within one has to learn the art of how to **meditate**; how to do breathwork so that *transcendence* becomes easier for everyone to know the secrets of the universe.

RETREAT (SOURCE GOOGLE)

Virtual orientation

A few days before the camp a virtual orientation was given
:

A 60 Hours of total silence was to be maintained during
the camp, with no phones, no communication between
participants no giving and sharing, and no eye contact.
There were special volunteers assigned who would help us
if we had any problems.

A single room separate for each was given to each one of
us. To keep it clean was our responsibility

All facilities were provided food, water, hot water bath,
blankets medicine, etc. Bells would ring according to when
a new session would start. During evening hours at 8 PM,
either a documentary or Guruji discourse would be shown
every day. Special instructions and task for the day were

given pre and post-sessions. A notebook was provided to keep notes etc.

CHAPTER THREE

BOOT CAMP Schedule

Time ------------------------ DESCRIPTION

4:30 a.m---------------- ----Jeera water (KITCHEN)

4.35 a.m ------------------(Assembly Hall) meditation

6.00a.m . -------------------- walk & (yoga)

7:00 a.m. --------------------Bath

7:30 a.m.-------------------- (Annapurna Hall)

8.00 a.m.-------------------- Activity hall

11:00 a.m. ----------------- (Front of temple area)

12:15 p.m ---------------------Lunch

2:00 p.m.---------------------- Meditation hall

5:00 p.m.---------------------- Evening dinner

6 .00 p.m ---------------------Meditation

7.00 p.m--------------------- Activity

7.30 p.m--------------------- Discourses

9.0 p.m--------------------- Rest (rooms)

Meditation

Venue Assembly Hall Day 1

We all assembled in the hall. A voice recording of guruji guided us all about the meditation that was to be done in this hall and special instructions were given regarding posture, breathwork, and concentration. we all did meditation for 90 minutes or so. Meditation was done in which awareness and How to Relax each and every body part was taught. the essence was the awareness and presence of our Body ...This meditation is similar to Yog Nidra Meditation done in all yoga classes. the afternoon and evening meditation were intense *i. e Ana Pana Sati Meditation and* profound.DAY 2 The meditation was transcendental meditation. after the meditation, we all assembled near the path area.

Walk Around the Temple Area

The Swami in charge of our group gave us instructions as we had to walk around the temple area in total **SILENCE** and come back and assemble in the Centre of the Park. In the park area, we all did exercises meant for each body part.

After this, a small Twin Heart Meditation (source youtube shortest twin heart)was shown to us to be done on a Daily Basis. This opens up the Heart Chakra. After & before a small lecture was delivered by the Swamiji in charge giving the significance, the importance of the activity.

The Essence of this Meditation was to Visualise a small Earth in front of us and bless each and everyone on this Planet Earth with Love Joy, peace Harmony Forgiveness and the Will to do Good.

A lot of Affirmations were also taught to us.

"I Affirm I pay gratitude to Mother Earth for all the gifts bestowed to us on this earth to live comfortably and happily fulfilling my Life Purpose in this Lifetime."

CHAPTER FIVE

Birth and Death

Activity 1

Each participant was given a paper and within 5 minutes duration, we had to think about our lives from Birth till Now... First, we had to put all our major events whatever we could remember on the Paper then we were assigned 2 minutes to share the paper with our Partner after this the partner was exchanged and the partner shared his experience with us.

Conclusion: this exercise concluded with that everybody underwent sufferings in their lives.

Activity 2

CRYING/LAUGHING

All had to lie down and then cry as if we were born today after this activity of crying about for 1 minute continuously everybody started laughing and now, we were asked to sit in our respective positions and laugh out loudly after this activity everybody's eyes were in tears ...

Conclusion joy and sorrow is the part of life's journey.

ACTIVITY 3 Saying it to the universe.

In this activity whatever our Current Problem was and whatever we were Struggling in life with: one by one we were asked to speak about our problem in the ears of a Monkey a Statue kept at the entrance of the temple. every participant spent around 4 to 5 minutes in this activity .By doing so we were conveying our deepest sorrow or problem to the Divine.

conclusion.In prayers, we speak to GOD & in meditation, GOD speaks to us.

CHAPTER SIX

Five Elements

Five Elements and their presence

Swamiji said after the Boot Camp was all over; Our problems will also come to an end as there will be challenges and we will have a New prescriptive. Life would not be the same again as we shift to higher consciousness with a new perspective all sufferings will be challenges and will be time-bound.

A small lecture about duality, the five elements of nature, and the consciousness around it created the universe. How every thought, action, and the feeling was building the universe bit by bit every day. The creation is vast and abundant and the information all these existed in the **akasha (ether)** and the primordial **sound** (OM) build the **frequency and vibration**s needed for evolving each moment. Each planet had a role to play in our lives as the earth revolves around the sun so do the microcosmos inside us also shift accordingly to the macro universe.

Every person has free will and intellect to do his duties (karmas) on a day-to-day basis ignorant about who is he in the real sense. is hidden from him since birth. One who becomes aware, and tries to awaken is the enlightened one like the BUDDHA. Every soul is potentially divine and is on their journey of discovery of this truth. Everything from knowledge to power and wealth is abundant in nature but out of ignorance we as humans operate from a lack of mindset.

All these are powerful insights one gains by coming to spiritual retreats like this. you as readers is not by chance you read this but GOD intended ME to give you all this clear message you are LIMITLESS, FORMLESS, BOUNDLESS, and existed as DIVINE ENERGY or SOUL(ATMA). The essence of PRANA is the life force that existed in each one of us known as AIR (VAYU) hence the pranayamas; bring awareness, the mind with the feelings, and the heart with the emotions all three align the mind, body, and soul.

Holy Water Dip

All were given a set of clothes to wear, first, we had to take a shower and wear the clothes, and then we were asked to take a Holy water dip in the two nearby Ponds. The ponds were named: the Suryakund and Chandrakund: Separate for Males and Females. After a Refreshing Bath, we all went for half an hour to our Cottage area, and then we were asked to Assemble for Breakfast in the Divine kitchen of Annapurna Hall.

Annapurna Hall

ACTIVITY 4

In the kitchen when we assembled: before eating we, all did a short Prayer to Thank Mother Earth for this

Sumptuous and pure food that gave us the energy to survive on this earth. A glass of water was given to every participant and also a meditation was taught to us on how to put affirmation into the glass and drink the water for Longevity Productivity and Vitality for our day-to-day needs.

Google. :(Water and Memory Masaru Emoto)

The Importance of a Pyramid was also given to us in how a pyramid helps to charge food and water in our daily lives. source Google for the importance of the pyramid in daily life.

Activity 5

A paper having various columns mentioning Grief, Guilt, Resentment Hatred, and Anger was given to us and we had to fill in the respective column's incident related to them. We were asked to keep this paper for later use. nearly 40 minutes were given for this activity as which is called the shadow self of us.

CHAPTER SEVEN

Mindfulness

Mindfulness activities were taught to us. How mindful are we? in our daily lives about the food we eat, our thoughts, and our actions? The essence of patience, calmness, and taking Breaks between the monotonous routine of our life was important.

How life evolved from the Sea to a plant kingdom to Animals and the world around us everybody learns in School: starts from early days at school. But how the whole Universe works on Auto Pilot Mode, nobody teaches us this in Classrooms. How the SOUL evolves in this human body as a vehicle is a discovery.

The whole science of the law of attraction was How Farmer grows a seed and the seed takes the time to become a Plant the Plant gives us the required Fruit in the Form of Wheat, Rice, Vegetables fruits Flowers, etc. all the universe is involved in either distributing or Consuming or production the fruits given by the Mother Earth

People involve in respective Professions like farming Transporting Administrative warehouses Agro industries, Textiles, etc. In this way, Money Laxmi flows from one hand to the other and the balance of the universe is maintained. Every minute manifestation is happening, the universe is evolving& expanding

Every Thought is manifested as Material.

ACTIVITY 7

Series of Subconscious mind exercises are done in this activity class to teach us about the various senses given to us like the sense of Taste, the purpose of Smell the sense of Touch, the importance of Hearing, and the sense of visualizing each and every object in our mind area. {panch bhutas, indreyas, khosahas}

New insights are very powerful exercises teach us and give lessons about various life problems.

CHAPTER EIGHT

Negative Emotions

Day1/ Activity 8

The Fire RITUAL

We all assembled near the Temple area where a big Havan Kund was kept each one was given a little offering (samagarhi). A lot other of flowers, ghee, fruits coconut, etc. were kept, near this. Then a lot of Mantra chanting was done and the offerings were one by one offered to the Agni Devta{Provider of heat, warmth, aggression, strength) Separate bonafide was made the letter of our negativity was torn apart and then each one of the participants took the Paper in which guilt and resentment had been written this paper was to be burnt in this fire. Nothing evolves into everything.

Conclusion. These activities show the technique of Letting go of all our negativity and negative emotions.

Past is Past one should not keep oneself holding on to the past for a longer time.

After this, we all felt very light-hearted. The best part was the ashes were added to potting plants so it added nutrition so in this way the exchange of energy happens.... There is nothing good or bad they are different emotions but doesn't serve us.

Death and life are the faces of the same coin. After this Activity and there was the essence of joy.

CHAPTER NINE

Raise Your Vibrations

Activity 9

Next time We all were taken to a dancing hall and music was playing on and everybody was asked to dance. The Best part was the music changed frequently .sometimes too slow and sometimes too fast and sometimes too sad music and sometimes so fast disco beats so everybody found it fun adjusting to the Tone of the music. These activities were done on both days. This activity showed us how music and sound could be so much fun and everybody had a good laugh. A roller coaster ride laugh. A world where suddenly everything goes wrong and sometimes it is so smooth in real life.

Activity 10

we all assembled in the hall again for a meditation this meditation was known as the Magical Library: after 45 minutes of doing this Meditation, the essence of the Meditation was to find our book in the Magical Library and remove all the negative pages, and rewrite our Destiny today... Everybody felt empowered after doing this meditation.

The significance of Goal setting I.e. what we actually wanted from life, in life and how we could serve this universe better was pre-explained. A lot of emphasis on goal setting was given, and why it is required. GOAL is a progressive realization of a desired means. the strangest secret (Earl Nightingale). A separate sheet was given for writing the goals and in various aspects physical, mental, spiritual

We had 90 min of Lunch break.

Activity 11

we all assembled in the hall again for a painting our own canvas. In this Activity, we were given colors to paint our lives as we desired. The Great art/picture of our life is similar to a vision board. after 45 minutes of doing this, the essence of the Activity was to find our picture full of various colors as above as below.

CHAPTER TEN

The Drama of Illusion

DISCOURSES GIVEN AT 8 P.M by GURUJI (BRIEF SUMMARY)

You live in a world of drama. The drama comes in many interesting packages the drama of family, the money drama, illness, the drama of your job, your family relationship, and the drama of your country.All the drama around you is an illusion and when you change your perception of the drama your experience of the drama changes.

you are here on this beautiful Earth to go Beyond the Illusion and Transcend your karma.

Everything is You and You are Everything.

What is reality?

To understand reality, you first need to understand Ego. We understand the world through our Ego and our brain. The Ego creates and connects to the illusion. The ego cannot see reality for what it truly is because it believes in the physical world and the physical senses. It believes that what the Eyes see is real and you should be fearful of anything you can't understand. EGO creates the line of separation between you and your Soul.

Karma is the Law of Attraction; your vibration is a reflection of your karma.

You are connected with all the people in your life because of your Karmic entanglement. You attract these people in your life to become completely aware. Of each experience in life according to the blueprint before your birth. To experience deep feelings you will need to take personal responsibility for yourself. This is not about achieving perfection: It is about cultivating self-realization which means looking at yourself and your actions honestly and without judgment. when you begin to recognize the Earth from the perspective of higher consciousness you start transforming. You always accumulate your karma always in your Physical Emotional and Mental bodies.

Your Aura's energy and colors are constantly moving.

It is not really about the color of your Aura which changes with circumstances and moods, it is about the clarity and brightness of the energy around you. Being caught in the wheel of Karma means you getting caught in the Illusion of the False Reality of the Self that you believe is who you really are. This is called Ego identity so many see the SELF as a Name, Job, or Family it has stories of hurt, anger, guilt, hatred, love fate, conflict, kindness, etc. but it is only the reflection of the truth of who you are.

The Ego's identity is an illusionary Self and can be changed and transformed. The Ego itself is a part of the Illusion what is the truth of who you really are? The truth of who you are is not Ego it is the whole divine self. when you clear your old patterns and you start to dissolve your Ego Identity then what you discover is the Divine in you or you a part of the divine. (book of knowledge)

Knowing is not Doing. Not knowing is Doing. Living is as living each day as a Miracle and Miracle is itself, Divine. Illusion is very abstract as the world you live in is dualistic. Since you live in a world of duality, it is easier to explain and understand things such as light, dark, old and new, up and down. The Ego helps to see your surroundings in a limited way and Ego and the senses tell you this is the only reality.

When you come to the Earth you start to feel separate from the Divine Love and you become caught in the Illusion of this linear, dualistic energy of the Lower planes, and this is called the Wheel of Karma or the Cycle of Life. The ego reality also includes or connects you to your perception, feelings, moods, and the environment, the past present, and the Future in store for You.

the Ego chases desires Craves for only Earth riches Money, Property, House Name Status, etc. (You become the ultimate consumer of your Ego.)The truth is that there is nothing outside of yourself that will completely fulfill your need for connection and love.

It is only through meditation and going within self Realisation you try to understand the difference between Illusion and reality. that is? You will awe stuck when you decipher the code of the matrix.Death is also an example of an illusion.

When you alter your state of Consciousness you change your reality. Karma is not punishment it is a beautiful opportunity to improve and change your life. Every discourse brings new insights into our life and the meaning of the discourse changes as our souls evolve, With more maturity, the truth unwinds and reveals new insights every time.

CHAPTER ELEVEN

Karma Releasing Ritual

THE RITUAL

Ingredients

white candle

Violet and Green candle (optional)

rock salt or any type of salt

Frequency once in 6 months.

Method

* First write down all the names of people whom you need to forgive.

* Write down the names of all people whom you have wronged.

*Write down the problems you are facing in life.

* Light the white candle and say the prayer.

Day: Saturday on New Moon, this activity can be done on Amavasya.

Prayer for Forgiveness.

* Dear God Goddesses and please send Archangel Metatron and millions of Angels to bless me in this Karma-releasing ritual. Dear God, Goddesses, Archangel Metatron, Jesus Juan Yin, and angels and millions of peace and forgiveness Angels. Please help me to completely and totally forgive myself and others.Please also help me to completely and totally forgive and forget the ones I have mentioned in the paper for their behavior towards me. Please help me with the Divine Light that part of me that is finding it difficult to forgive them. I also sincerely request to be forgiven completely for any action, words, thoughts, or deeds that have cost any pain or resentment to anyone living or dead in all directions of time across lifetimes. Please help me to become compassionate towards other people and myself This or Better.

Thank you Thank you Thank you. NOW tear the paper keep it on a plate put salt over it and put it in the dustbin; wash the plate.

What an easy way to forgive others. Through this activity, everyone experienced FREEDOM from our self-created prison, our own shackles of false mind illusion.

How EGO pays its game of big & small. we all felt as if a heavy burden just went away as light as a bird. all was in front of us how we acted when this incident happened and calendars changed but the wound of not forgiving someone was still fresh in our hearts.

ACTIVITY 9 & 11 were repeated after this for day 2 also

DANCING & PAINTING brought new zeal, and joy, now we actively participated with more joy now.

CHAPTER TWELVE

Divine YOU

DAY2 ASSEMBLY HALL

I am sharing a Beautiful Divine Future You Meditation, which will help you to deeply Relax and come out of this meditation with deep sense of Positive feelings and essence of Divinity , Power of Joy and happiness in You.

This Meditation will help you to bring peace and Bliss.

To create the feelings of positive sensation before doing this exercise drink water and relax yourself completely and sit comfortably.

Sit comfortably and imagine that you see your image in front of You at a fair distance.

Sitting here now...... Imagine making the images as attractive you want.

Imagine the Divine You in this image has learnt how to be beautiful how to dress elegantly with grace...

See the Divine you enjoying the love of this life,

see how he/she looks compassionate, positive, full of kindness, full of love ...

make those pictures and Panoramic...

See the Divine you being Rich, Exuberant Passionate, Knowledgeable,

that serves the humanity ...

giving some money in charity...

doing all that is good for highest good....

Imagine Divine You full of health, Vitality Energy having a deep sense of peace and Bliss within ...

The Divine you as the Divine child of the Divine....

Imagine The Divine you following all the commands given by the Divine to live a life full of Prosperity Peace Satisfaction and Contentment...

See the attractive Visuals.

Imagine some significant people are appreciating....

Listen to the attractive Visuals and hearing the Sounds of Appreciation experience the true feelings that are developing in your body...

imagine a life book in which appreciation about your feedbacks, newspapers and the medias clips about you...

you can add number of visuals in this picture the number of places where you have given or delivered your speeches ....

imagine places where you have taken workshops and seminars and spreading your message to the world ....

Imagine a loving White pure light inside you that is helping you with each day to Progress...

with this divinity inside You...

Finally make the picture bright and imagine that you are getting up from here and going there in front of the Divine You...

Imagine You are integrating with the Divine You and adopting all The Wonderful images on Your Mental Screen...

Now You and Divine You are One....

repeat this exercise the number of times to get better results

start acting like Now... don't wait for tomorrow it never comes.

Get assured that you are on the right path and enjoying the milestones You have created.

Be flexible to change your approach till you get what to have desired and this keeps you going towards your Goals.

This is your success Formulae.

CHAPTER THIRTEEN

Seven Chakras

Practice Chakra meditation :

There are basically 7 Chakras in the human body and each serves as a Nexus or a point of energy to vitalize the human body. Carrying the energy are Nadis similar to nerves. This vast network of nadis empties into chakras that sit along a central system. The Central channel having Sushumna has two smaller channels (ida and the Pingla) all three align along the spiral Column. As the Kundalini Rises Special Powers are activated.

Activity 6

In the Boot Camp, the participants were taught Breathwork, yoga positions, and Pranayama to release negativity associated with each that was holding onto to them. certain (Beej mantras) mantras associated with each were taught to us. Intuitions are God's gifts in order to nurture this superpower, one has to meditate.

seven chakras (VIBGYOR)

Each chakra is a nodal point and is related to a color, a planet, a salt, a quality, a crystal, a weekday, an emotion, and a description, and a detailed video was shown on how it affects our daily activities.

CHAPTER FOURTEEN

Angels Our Guardians

Angels and the Angelic realm.

Angels are Celestial Beings working the closest with Humans. There are many kinds of Angels including the Guardian's angels. Cultivating an open mind will help us to communicate with the Angels.

One has to let go of any Bias or Prejudice which may block the Signs and signals of angels' Presence.If ever we witness a person Saving the life of a Human Being in the Right Place at the Right Time it is actually witnessing an Angel performing a miracle.

Practice Gratitude and Recognizing the Small Things as blessings in life instead of troubles When We Are Grateful for all that we have. and giving a thank you or a smile helps us to raise our vibrations. This helps us to get more connected to this Angelic Realm raising the vibration becomes a powerful force for attracting good people events things and Angels into our lives.

Angels want to work with the help of our experience. They help us so that we experience heaven on earth.

Gratitude fosters hope and the belief that the impossible can be possible. As we expand our Awareness of possibility, we increase our opportunities to experience good things in our life.

Angel helps us to create Legacy and masterpieces in our lives.Very powerful techniques were taught to invoke ANGELS

CHAPTER FIFTEEN

The SOUL Purpose

DISCOURSE (BRIEF SUMMARY)

The misconception about soul purpose in the Spiritual community is that soul has come here to do Something. The Truth is that Life's purpose is about how you live your life and how you express your soul, Purpose. Soul purpose isn't about Doing it is about Being. The soul's purpose is to be more in alignment with who we truly are. Be connected, be compassionate, and serve the world. The reason so many people are unhappy in their Jobs or life is that they aren't listening to the Soul Voice. Your Soul wants to express who you are being, which is more important than what you are doing.

Everyone's, yes, I mean Everyone's Soul purpose is the same. If every person takes 100% responsibility for his life, then life becomes easier and the experience becomes fuller of Inner joy peace and feelings of Oneness and Expansion. When we cover **ourselves in the blanket of shame guilt, sadness, anger, and resentment and see the World as a dark place and the people of earth as bad, then we are**

buying into this Illusion.

Everyone's Soul's Purpose is to transcend the Illusion and the Ego's delusion, to express Love, and to become the energy of Equanimity.

<u>*This Illusion keeps us stuck in fear, anger, and guilt.*</u>

When we start to recognize that we are living in an illusion then there is no right or wrong, good or bad, we will learn to forgive, and let go of anger and sadness. True transformation happens when we no longer see the world in an angry, sad, or bitter way. You start to perceive what happens to yourself and others' love and compassion. You see the bigger picture you are less likely to fight argue or withdraw.

Equanimity is when we feel love and compassion while in the middle of a chaotic situation.

when we call negative experiences lessons but they are only experiences. This experience will never upset us if We Don't React. **then it is more about Self Realization and Less about the lessons.** As Lessons of life once it is done the same experience becomes a part of Karma. knowing oneself so intimately is the key to self-realization and personal development. In the Spiritual journey when we see the world with higher consciousness recognize our true selves and forgive others. easily then this state of high consciousness brings bliss, Self-Love inner joy expansion, and compassion for all in the whole world.

CHAPTER SIXTEEN

Finding Passion

DISCOURSE 2 DAY 2 (Brief summary)

Therefore, even when you are in a job, you can learn skills to become Singer, Actor, Comedian Author, Trainer Life Coach Public Speaker Taro Card Reader Numerologist. (anything you wanted to be in childhood or you are passionate about). Once you promote yourself and your skill you become a Celebrity. It will convert you into a brand and open a lot of resources of money.

Exercise.

Find a comfortable place to spend some time with yourself to explore what best you can do to add value to the life of people. What you can do that people will like. Explore which area of being Entrepreneur suits you well. Explore how you see yourself on the life Time Line. Explore your core skills. Explore what gives you a feeling of accomplishment and satisfaction.

Write your Health, Wealth, Spiritual and Intellectual Goals! what are your short-term and long-term Goals? Explore what brings you more Appreciation from people and from Within as well in your life. Now imagine that You are very happy and satisfied because you have accomplished something Unique in your life.

Imagine you have completed 100 years of your age now explore what it that you have done in your life that makes you happy and satisfied this can be your Purpose in Life. All the best for your future endeavors in life. This brings you to the end of the Day 2 program.

We all were provided a Diary to write all our Goals, a bucket list, and a set of rituals to do be done on an everyday basis. A prasad bag was also given. I could now CorrelateStrange are the ways of the Divine that this bag brought me here and more the gifts bestowed upon me...I had a Rapid Inner transformation ...

I learnt finally How to get rid of the Ego hassles for my highest level of good.

How every negative thought, word, or action was CANCEL DELETE ERASE (magical switch words) was for me. Divine come now, Divine Protect me now Divine Heal me Now. (chant these switch word)

CHAPTER SEVENTEEN

The Quest

Discourse

Guruji started his usual discourse with a story:

The best example Guruji says that one should learn from Thomas Alva Edison in making of the electric bulb that he failed 999 times but he never gave up. "All this was possible; Only after the bulb was invented .Today we have the electricity, light and also a whole new world of Technology, artificial intelligence and so on.....

Guruji asked how many of you read about the Bhagavad Gita?Similarly Bhagavad Gita has all the answers about our Life.In the Gita God himself explains& tells Arjuna about the real Self, the Ego Self and the Higher Self.Every person who is born today will die one day; but essence of Soul will be continuing the journey till it learns the Lessons of life. One who surrenders to the Universal Divine Energy will only attain Salvation.It is like the salt Doll who tries to fathom the Sea but only to realize that it is the part of the same Ocean when it jumps into the seaThe moment you realize this a whole new word of possibilities open up.Throughout one person's lifetime he spends his life in the Worldly Environment collects and accumulates Wealth For his Family.... . In doing so he forgets about he and himself.

Guruji further adds that Suffering is Optional. in this world because of ignorance. Human ignorance brings suffering ....when the Quest begins, he gains the knowledge (Gyan) and performs his duties (Karma). He finally surrenders when he cannot find answers, he becomes a devotee (Devotion). He attains Salvation in his own place/ Time zone. For all this to happen Ignorance has to turn into illumination.

One has to increase one Energy.

"How to do that? "

so here comes the Healers and other modalities which increase Energy. Creativity comes into the picture even with painting and music. You have to remain always Happy in every moment of Life. in this vibrational Plane. when you surrender then you become one with the Supreme God. You invite miracles into your life as the cosmic energy becomes Quantum Field. Hence Everything is possible ...Manifestation is always there happening every moment now you align yourself with the universe such that you start faking your reality and with correct imagination and visualization you create a magnificent, abundant, wealthy, healthy life for yourself. now every thing that happens in Your Life you feel is a MIRACLE!

It becomes magical but only A few Souls feel Magic happening in their lives because of their EGO Self and time. So, it is said that Life is a journey where one learns the lessons of Life. when the mind becomes calm and quiet it will be in the Quest mode and will try to find out "who am I? " Once he figures out when he himself gets all the answers until then Manifestation is not decoded.

All The Spiritual teachers try to say the same truth according to their own circumstances, their time zone, and their State of Mind in their respective Era. Truth is one and universal but books and explanations are many depending on one's realization according to their mindset.

The conclusion is that is why there are so many books on Self Growth, Creativity, Healing spirituality etc.

This brings us to the end of the 2 days Retreat Program Everybody is on their Life Journey and Guruji advised us today "Do not row an anchored boat."..

CHAPTER EIGHTEEN

Who am I?

Myself Anjana Baliga, I use Angel cards and Akashic Records, as it is the easiest way to Transcend life: and raise our vibrations ...empowering people from all walks of life. I as the Akashic Record Reader and a Tarot card reader help people deal with their Emotional, Mental, and Physical problems.

After this camp (2020) since then; I learned new skills in occult sciences, tarot reading, NLP, Hypnotherapy, Akashic records, Cartomancy, Numerology, Drowsing, Past life regression, Life coaching, public speaking, etc.

These records on the Quantum Field are pure consciousness. and sometimes called Oneness, in the akashic library. These records hold not only information from our planet but the whole Cosmos as well. Everything around us including the most subtle energy resides here.

It contains all the information, everything that has happened in all planes up till now. By accessing Akashic Records with the permission of the Client one can access and get more information and heal them from anywhere. I feel highly blessed to be blessed by Angels and be the chosen One to read the Akashic records. This requires a lot of practice and years of hard work meditation and building upon the intuition to perceive things.

I offer My Greatest gratitude and open My Heart ♥And Feel oneness and unconditional love.

Thanks for the gifts bestowed to me by the Divine to serve this world.

I thank the divinity in me and bow down to the divine in you all. If you find the content of this book useful ; Please share this book with friends and family.

Anjana Baliga's artistic and eclectic interest combined with a desire to be a lifelong learner has driven her to study and teach these Akashic Records /Tarot cards. {Raider Waite Tarot card }readings to all those who are passionate Learners like her. .... KUSHALI (Mentor)

CHAPTER NINETEEN

WORKBOOK

Anjana Baliga: recollect the words Tony Robinson says that the quality of your life depends upon the quality of questions you ask yourself on a day-to-day basis.

So here is a list of Questions. Please ponder over them and sincerely try answering them. This is a Mini Workbook, this workbook will help you to change your mindset and achieve success in life and it will also open new doors of new ideas in your life.

Ponder over these questions over &over again to achieve success and try answering them.

- From what mindset are you operating; Is it a Champion /victor mindset or a victim or a loser mindset?

- . Write down your single most goal and on a scale of 1 to 10 write how committed are you to achieving it.

- if you had just 24 hours to live what would be the three most important things you would like to do before you leave this world?

- If you had just 60 seconds recollect what are the three most important lessons you learned in this lifetime.

- Write 10 things you know and check if are they facts or true.

  If the sun rises in the East is it a fact? Yes or No.
  Are you a nice person is it truth or fact?

- Keep asking yourself a critical question am I growing or Dying? if you are not dying then what is that you are doing to keep yourself growing?

- Write a list of 10 beliefs that you have gathered since your childhood if someone says there is a huge block regarding your Finance, question yourself about how huge is it.?
- or ask if the block is huge compared to what? You will arrive at your answer.

- Ask five people what they have to say about your conduct ask your family /friends and your office persons on a scale of 1 to 10 to check it how close they are.
- Analyze Do they really know you or do you know yourself better?

- Why does it hurt your ego when somebody asks you to corporate with their project?

- Think about your life journey and can you thank people who have helped you in this journey so far for what they have done for you? name them and the events.

- Can you avoid gossip for a day and check whether it has really helped you to gain the right time?

- Check your mood springs every 6 hours does it swing often or there is a pattern to it?

- Do you need often validation from others?

- if you speak the truth and still people say" He is out of his Minds today" how comfortable are you ?
- On a day to day basis find out what is this stress about and how is it affecting your happiness ?

- keep a quote or a mental toughness advice and see how you cope with it.

- Keep a coach and ask him for his advice so that you can ponder over your own ideas and find a quick solution.

- It is said that help is just a hand away try calling someone and find the solution for your problem.

- Ponder quickly about the answer you get in completion of your goals .check how close you are.

- How many times you failed in life. ? Don't forget Addison tried 999ways bulb didn't work out. Have you tried at least ten times before giving up.

- If the problem seems to be a mountain try changing it into a ice ball. what was yours?

- when you assign someone some work on a scale of 1 to 10 what is your expectations from them .

- on the scale of 1 to 10 find out how much you love yourself and why you feel bad when somebody talks something against you .

- write at least 20 things that you love about yourself find out what you love doing can it bring you any money?
- Are others doing the same thing and earning from it .

- if you ever failed at something find out what are the lessons learnt from these failures.
- if Addison failed 999 times how many times did you feel as a winner in the past 30days.

- Develop your communication skill and write a script to sell a pen to your friend and see whether it works. Were you successful in creating the need.

- What did you gain, we're you able to analyze customer pain points.

- Practice mindfulness activities with the food everyday as you eat your lunch; count your blessings and to all the ingredients that is served to you from breakfast to dinner.

- Try finding how are humanity is connected to procure, manufacturer And deliver these ingredients.

- On a day to day basis thank the food and find out is it carbohydrate or a protein rich food you are eating .

- check the food while having lunch and dinner check whether it is man made sealed in Packets or plant based raw food.. Try avoiding the packet as it contains preservatives.

- Always put an intention to the water before you drink. State your intentions what you want to be in future like I am young, energetic, highly productive etc.

- it it is said that you are an average of five people, have you found those 5 people?

- when someone does not recognise your work how guilty on a scale of 1 to 10 you feel?

- start patting your back and yourself for the good you do everyday and praising yourself today .

- Does it feel good validating yourself if yes keep doing it daily..

- Give yourself a foot massage and a head massage today, both provide direction and movement in life. Give equal importance to both..

- Try the 6 phase meditation by mindvalley and continue till you really see manifestation happening..

- Try walking a mile from YouTube do everyday it takes 15minutes. ON a scale of 1 to 10 how to do feel energy wise after doing it?

- Try finding why 432hz is the healing frequency in the universe.

- What are bad habits you want to give up. Don't forget to replace them with healthy ones.

- Try dancing to a tune and listen to music everyday on a scale of 1to 10 observe the difference

- On a Scale of 1 to 10 how useful I was delivering you the content

- if you feel this book has really help you in any way please put a review on Amazon/ Flipkart or Notion price from where did you buy the book.

- It is said that sharing is caring and if you feel that your friends and family should benefit by reading this book do share with more people

- I am on a mission to create more healers and more coaches so that they can empower other people to be financially free... Are you future READY .?

About The Author

Full of compassion versatile electronic engineer an author, a writer, a motivational speaker a G.S.B., Brahmin convent educated now a Spiritual life coach. Anjana Baliga is a certified spiritual life coach and reader of Akashic records connected to the Divine.

She is a certified NLP practitioner, hypnotherapist, Life coach, Lama Fera healer, Cognitive Behavior Therapist, Angel therapist, and Avid reader of Tarot and playing cards.

Akashic records are the blueprint of your soul. It is a Soul book; a living database that contains not only the current information but past lifetimes' Karmic baggage, Soul ties, and Soul contracts. She has more than 5 years of experience working with clients to clear negative patterns; to understand who they are at a Soul level. she provides mediumship readings, Akashic records, and Tarot readings. she provides Remedies and healings so the client can live a life full of peace joy, harmony, and bliss